How to Talk to Anyone

51 Easy Conversation Topics You Can Use to Talk to Anyone Effortlessly

James W. Williams

© Copyright 2018

All rights reserved.

The content contained within this book may not be reproduced, duplicated or transmitted without direct written permission from the author or the publisher.

Under no circumstances will any blame or legal responsibility be held against the publisher, or author, for any damages, reparation, or monetary loss due to the information contained within this book. Either directly or indirectly.

Legal Notice:

This book is copyright protected. This book is only for personal use. You cannot amend, distribute, sell, use, quote or paraphrase any part, or the content within this book, without the consent of the author or publisher.

Disclaimer Notice:

Please note the information contained within this document is for educational and entertainment purposes only. All effort has been executed to present accurate, up to date, and reliable, complete information. No warranties of any kind are declared or implied. Readers acknowledge that the author is not engaging in the rendering of legal, financial, medical or professional advice. The content within this book has been derived from various sources. Please consult a licensed professional before attempting any techniques outlined in this book.

By reading this document, the reader agrees that under no circumstances is the author responsible for any losses, direct or indirect, which are incurred as a result of the use of information contained within this document, including, but not limited to, — errors, omissions, or inaccuracies.

Table Of Contents

Introduction 9

Chapter One: Communication and Development 12

Chapter Two: Do's and Don'ts: Basic Guide to Good and Proper Conversations 21

    You 22
        Don't steal all the spotlight 22
        It's not all about You 23
        Empathy is Everything 24
        Be a Conduit rather than an Endpoint 25
        Raise your Energy 26
        Be an Empty Vessel 27

    Conversation 27
        Keep it Flexible 28
        Don't Drop the Small Talk 28
        Watch Out for Sensitive Topics 29

    People 30
        Check the Non-Verbal Signs 30

Chapter Three: The Best 51: Topics to Make Easy and Interesting Conversations 32

Opener/Starter 33
   Killer Starters/Openers 33

Details/Fillers 35

Ender/Exit 42

Art of Small Talk 44
   Weather 45
   People 46
   Sceneries 47
   Events/Seasons 48
   Personal Experiences/Details 48
   Common Ground 49
   Current Events 50
   Work 51
   Sports/Games 51
   Music 52
   Hobbies and Crafts 53
   World Issues 54
   Anything Under the Sun 55

Chapter Four: Flex Your Conversation Muscles 56

First-Name Basis 56

Just Yes or No is a No-no 57

Be Natural 57

Conclusion: Going Beyond with the Power of Conversation 59

    Emotion 60

    Expertise 60

    Positional Power 61

    Interaction 61

Thank you! 63

Your Free Gift

As a way of saying thanks for your purchase, I wanted to offer you a free bonus E-book called ***Bulletproof Confidence Checklist*** exclusive to the readers of this book.

To get instant access just go to:

https://theartofmastery.com/confidence/

Inside the book, you will discover:

- What is shyness & social anxiety, and the psychology behind it
- Simple yet powerful strategies for overcoming social anxiety
- Breakdown of the traits of what makes a confident person

- Traits you must DESTROY if you want to become confident
- Easy techniques you can implement TODAY to keep the conversation flowing
- Confidence checklist to ensure you're on the right path of self-development

Introduction

How often do you go out and meet people? Do you have problems speaking with strangers, especially during office parties and events you can't avoid attending? Do you get awkward in groups? Cat always got your tongue? You might be as introvert as the next person but talking with people is something you cannot possibly run from every single time. Humans, as social beings, are biologically wired to communicate. Language and communication play a key role in our survival and development.

Not to dwell so much on the biological and social importance of communication though, it is a truth well-known that conversing with people, especially strangers doesn't come as easily for all of us. This doesn't mean, however, that being a great and much-remembered conversationalist is an elusive dream. On the contrary, the talent for speaking is a work in progress that is not so different from learning to play the piano or starting a new hobby like dancing or stitching. It's a skill that requires practice, and surely some trial and error inserted here and there.

This book will be your headstart – a path to becoming the charismatic, interesting, and smart conversationalist who can talk with confidence with anyone, at any setting or event. It provides practical tips, and some exercises to build and strengthen your conversation muscles. Aside from the do's and don'ts you can use as a guideline of a sort in conversing, this book also shows a total of 51 topics for conversation that will definitely hook the people you talk with and make you the unforgettable guy or gal before you leave the party.

Applying the principles of this book in real life may be every bit of a challenge because the hardest part of the journey is breaking the ice hindering you from standing smoothly on the starting line. Even as you successfully make the first step and take the journey, challenges and failures will continue rocking your boat. However, not moving forward will make you a stagnant witness that remains in one place while the rest of the world changes and evolves. That is a worse scenario even if you try to look at it at every different angle. Don't be left behind! Swallow down that nervousness and flex your conversation muscles. This book will not fail you on the basics, but rather push you a little towards the center stage. Don't be afraid to get some of the spotlight for yourself.

Talk. Get to know people. BE KNOWN.

Chapter One: Communication and Development

Communication is a crucial part of a person's social development. The ability to construct words into meaningful communication is a natural skill that distinguishes us from other mammals, establishing our superior intelligence as overall species. Language and communication shape the intelligence and social skills of the speaker and the people he/she interacts with. Culture and social norms in a specific community are also defined by language. For instance, instilling a set of rules and behavioral standards at a very young age influences a person's development as a unique individual with certain traits, behavior, decision-making strategies, skills, and beliefs. It is no surprise to find these components similar to those of succeeding generations, as they are passed from parents to children.

Language and communication are also key players in emotional development. Through conversation and regular interaction with other people, a person learns not only the right words to express ideas and feelings, but also nonverbal indicators such as gestures, tone, and facial expressions that give more meaning to what is being said. Emotions are mostly expressed nonverbally through facial expressions, eye contact, and body language, but they are more understood by other people when putting words to them. Experiences made during conversations help develop empathy and social skills that are not necessarily taught and learned in books, such as analyzing subtexts and hidden meanings and appropriately responding to them in words and ways that are within the confines of what is proper and socially acceptable. Ultimately, development of cognitive, emotional, and social skills nurtures a person's growth and ability to build and sustain relationships.

Three Pillars of Communication

There are three (3) main pillars of communication every person needs to take to heart. These are non-verbal communication, conversation skills, and assertiveness.

Non-verbal Communication

Ever heard the saying, "Words are wind?" We may say things that we don't really mean. Words can be easily used to lie, control, and manipulate. They are powerful weapons, and they can be dangerous. Non-verbal signs, instinctual gestures, and body language, on the other hand, are just as powerful, or maybe even more. Words can be diverted from their true meaning, but non-verbal gestures are difficult to fake. Oftentimes, they speak more honestly than what the mouth says and therefore are more effective in putting messages across to people. To be a better conversationalist, you should watch out for hand gestures, eye contact, and facial expressions, and learn to divulge their meanings.

Communication Skills

The strongest indicator of a good conversationalist is his/her skills in communicating, not only based on how good or right he/she utilizes words to get the most desired responses from the people being talked to, but also by how he/she maintains the conversation smooth and going.

Assertiveness

Being assertive doesn't necessarily mean taking all the spotlight and being selfish in directing conversations to wherever you want without considering the feelings of other people. On the contrary, assertiveness means being honest with your own feelings, needs, ideas and wants, yet being mindful of other people's needs and opinions at the same time. Assertiveness is not settling for passive conversation, wherein you hold yourself back. Conversation is give and take, where everyone learns and grows together.

Conversing easily and being loved for it is a skill that takes a lot of practice, and even embarrassing life anecdotes. It's part of the learning curve. It's true that there are people who were born with charisma and silver tongue, but this doesn't mean that people who aren't genetically gifted with words can't be a good or exceptional conversationalist. Anyone can, but like all paths leading to grander things, there are obstacles on the way.

Fear

One of the obstacles that limit a person from being a confident speaker is fear. Some of the thoughts that fuel such fear are being judged wrongly by other people, embarrassing the self, causing misunderstanding, and unintentionally hurting others. Fear and the thoughts or events that trigger it are wired to past experiences. It is very difficult to overcome something that has been imprinted in our system. As the saying goes, "old habits die hard." Letting go of the fear that hinders you from speaking easily to others may be a huge iceberg that's impossible to even crack, but at least you can try to mellow it down to a comfortable level. How?

Rate Your Fear

Fear isn't too abstract to be assessed, especially on a personal level. Without too much thinking and drama on the backdrop, nobody knows you more than yourself. You can rate your fear based on how strong you feel it, and this is the first step to trying to control it if overcoming it seems impossible, or at least impossible at the moment. Let's try this with the following questions:

What makes you so afraid or nervous about talking to people?

When did you start having such fear? What happened back then that possibly developed your fear of talking to people?

What are the other elements you remember from that time, e.g. people, sounds, surroundings, etc?

When was the last time you felt the same fear or been in a situation very similar to the first one when your fear was triggered? What did you do? Who were you with? How did it end?

Ask these questions to yourself and feel your fear. On a scale of 0 – 10, how afraid are you? On a scale of 0 – 10, how do you think you will fare if you are in the same situation again? By evaluating the level of your fear, you establish a baseline from which you can start working from. It's difficult to assess how much effort you would invest in if you don't have a point of reference. The target is to try to get further from this baseline bit by bit.

Dwell on It

When you repeatedly find yourself in the same situation, the drill becomes cumbersome and boring. It's the same with fear. If you are faced with the same fear over and over again, chances are your original fear diminishes, because somehow, you are ready and prepared to tackle it.

This is especially true if you've somehow gained the knowledge on how to combat it. The repeated process is part of a learning curve, remember?

However, this step is a long stretch, so put the test on an imaginary scenario. Imagine yourself in the same situation that raises your fear. In this setting, you have the choices to act differently. How would you respond to it this time? What do you think will be the better course of action? Do you feel empowered this time? If you do, that's the first indicator that you're ready to take on the challenge of facing your fear in real life circumstances. You already have an idea on how to better act, and perhaps get a more desirable outcome. Always remember that fear is driven by your thoughts, and if you redirect your thoughts towards a path that you prefer, then you can put your fear to a place where you want it – inside a box where you can contain and control it.

Face It

You know more about your fear now and have some ideas on how to redirect it or limit its grip on your nerves. You're now much more equipped on handling it. The final stage to test your mettle in the real world. Go to a public event. Grab the opportunity to be in a setting where speaking with strangers is inevitable. Approach a few and begin with your first test.

Chapter Two: Do's and Don'ts: Basic Guide to Good and Proper Conversations

The path to becoming an exceptional conversationalist is an art in the making. Like all works of art, there are basics to follow, guidelines to adhere to, before creating your very own masterpiece. Yes, conversations are supposed to be flexible. They take different shapes and traverse various routes, depending on the people controlling them. However, basic etiquette to proper conversing exists, and it would do you good to keep them in mind and practice all the time. The basic guide of good and proper conversation is defined by the following setup.

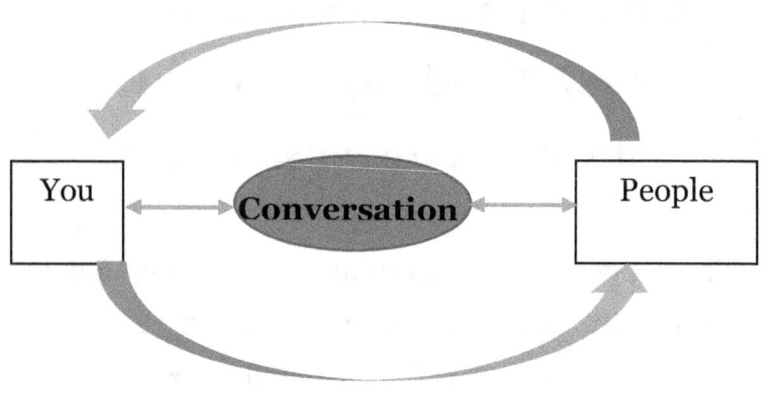

You

This set of rules is specifically for you – your actions, attitude, and behavior.

Don't steal all the spotlight.

People normally want to be the center of attention - the most interesting, the funniest, the most charismatic, the best guy/gal in the room. This is a trap – a bog of pride that will eventually push you under. While it's totally okay (sort of) to sometimes grab the spotlight when you're talking with family and close friends, the same won't cut it when you're rowing the boat on strange waters. Humans can be conceited peacocks. We want to leave a good impression wherever we go, especially in a company of strangers who have the potential to become new acquaintances or good friends, depending on how they strike that spark with you. Being a bragger or a know-it-all, typically anyone with humongous head and ego will definitely gain you enemies rather than friends.

It's not all about You.

If you think that a rip in your jeans or a wine stain on your white blouse will gain the attention and sniggers of all the people in the room, think again. Remember that in unfamiliar waters, the first and foremost in people's mind and concern is their own selves. They're probably more worried about how they will make the best impression at a party of people. With that running along the larger chunk of their brain, don't ever think that they have time to look at your shirt and pick on you for it. If you, however, find yourself being noticed for that rip or stain or whatever wardrobe malfunction, then perhaps you have your clumsiness and misfortune as starting topic for conversation and possible source of friendly laughter with strangers. This feat is quite tricky though, and you must have that cool sense of humor under your sleeves to perfectly ace it.

Empathy is Everything.

Putting yourself in someone else's shoes always gain appreciation, especially from strangers who don't have a gauge to measure you with, except the impressions they have of you on the first meeting. For instance, if the topic is a sensitive one, and you find yourself in the side of the fence opposite to that of the person you're talking to, be the proverbial cucumber and keep your horses down. You don't have to be passive, you just have to take the time to listen and see different points of view in the eyes of their believer. Even when you disagree, be courteous and kind about it. Don't lose your hair if you find yourself butting heads with an impenetrable wall of opinion. You'll have that luck of meeting some people who think and act like the world revolves around them. Be the bigger person. Part from them with unerring politeness, and a warm smile.

Be a Conduit rather than an Endpoint.

People who stay in the middle and make effort to understand their surroundings and the people in it are much more remembered in a positive way. There is this trick that most likable people have mastered to make them unforgettable. It's the ability to go with the waves of conversation and give way for other people to shine. I know someone who never fails to charm his way in the crowd. His secret? He lets the other person talk more about himself, and he makes more opportunities for that person to talk by directing the conversation toward a shared area of interest. He never acts like a doormat, no. The man is just so open-minded that other people's interest spikes his own, and he asks questions to learn more and keep the conversation flowing.

Raise your Energy.

The magic word: ENTHUSIASM. When you feel and act enthused, it is easy to infect people with positive energy; much more if you set the energy bar higher. Remember that people want to talk about themselves. Being interested and acting like it when they do so will endear you to them. Again, there should be a balance. You don't have to forget your own opinions and desire to be known. You should also give details about yourself when the opportunity presents itself, but stay within a zone of shared interest or similar topic so as not to steal someone else's thunder.

Be an Empty Vessel.

The world has more questions than answers. When unsure of what topics to tackle to keep the conversation flowing, ask questions. Think of yourself as an empty cup waiting to be filled to the brim with new information. Asking questions can also up your endearment points because it shows your interest and enthusiasm about the people you're talking to, and your sincere want to really know them.

Conversation

Conversation, or how they're supposed to unravel, is not easy to control, and frankly, it shouldn't be. That's the fun in it – the element of surprise and sense of adventure are gifts you can unwrap with your conversation partner. Still, there are rules that proper conversation has to live by, and conversationists need to adhere to. Conversations need to be harmonious, balanced, and positive for all parties involved. They also have to stay within the confines of social standards to avoid offending or insulting anyone.

Keep it Flexible.

Conversation is like a meandering river. It can change abruptly, in direction, pace, or both. It can stop at one point. Interruptions happen, but they shouldn't discourage you from continuing where you left off, or start an altogether new topic. The trick is to be an instrument of flow, and not an obstacle. Remember the second rule for you: it's not all about you.

Don't Drop the Small Talk.

A lot of people underestimate the power of small

talk. They think it too shallow or petty, and absolutely dispensable. They want to jump over the first steps and deal with the real thing immediately. Small talk is an effective starting point – an opportunity to build the conversation into something more and deeper. It provides the stage for first impressions, and for people to be acquainted. It is a chance to be well-liked from the very start.

Watch Out for Sensitive Topics.

Sensitive issues like religion, politics, and death are absolutely no-go when conversing with people for the first time. These topics have so much personal bias, and unless you're in a company of friends or people you're close to, they're not safe grounds.

People

There are a lot of helpful things you can find if you manage to observe carefully the people you're talking to. The subtle movements and expressions can tell you if the conversation is successfully and smoothly progressing. What your conversation partner does helps you determine the best ways to respond.

Check the Non-Verbal Signs.

Does your conversation partner maintain eye contact when speaking with you? Is his/her stance away from you? Are his/her arms crossed in the chest? Does he/she yawn frequently? Does he/she often look away from you when you're speaking? These are indicators of the success or failure of your conversation with someone. If the stance, eye contact, and movement or small fidgets of the person you're talking to are always away from you, that person is not interested in how your conversation is progressing and wants to get away from you as soon as the opportunity permits it. If there is yawning, it's highly likely that you bore the person. Seeing these signs, you're now faced with two choices: redirect the whole conversation towards something more interesting for the person, or drop the whole thing and gracefully part ways. You'll know how to properly react by evaluating non-verbal cues and reading words' subtexts.

Chapter Three: The Best 51: Topics to Make Easy and Interesting Conversations

A good conversation proceeds as follows:

Opener/Starter ➔ Details and Filler ➔ Ender/Exit

The opener/starter is the introduction phase. The details and the filler comprise the body of the whole conversation. It doesn't mean that the discussion at this stage of conversation traverses a single topic. Like spokes in a wheel, the procession of the conversation can go to different directions. The ender is the final say. It's not a wrap-up per se, but this is where the amicable parting of ways happens, and final impression sets in.

Opener/Starter

The most challenging part of a conversation is the opener. Oftentimes, we find ourselves struggling to strike a conversation because we don't know where to start. The opener can make or break the whole conversation process, because this might be the only chance you have to grab your prospect's attention and make a good impression. The opener is the building point of the whole conversation. Before asking any question, however, do the courtesy of **introducing yourself first**.

Killer Starters/Openers

Killer starters should be far more interesting than cliché questions such as "Where are you from" or "What do you think will be the weather tomorrow?" For an easier topic, be straightforward in asking the person about any interesting event that highlights his/her day or week, or talking about the event or place where both of you are currently at. Using your environment and surroundings to choose possible opener topics is easier and less likely to fail, compared to asking personal questions right off the bat. The following are good examples:

1. Hi, I'm _____. How do you do?

2. Do you know the host/event organizer?

3. This event is so _____. Have you ever been to a similar event before?

4. What brings you to this event by the way?

5. This place is _____. I have been to _____ with a _____ similar to this. Where did you come from/Where do you live by the way?

6. Well, the hor d'ouvres is _____! Did you like/hate it, too? What did you like/hate best/least?

7. What do you do/What's your job?

Details/Fillers

This stage of the conversation is where you can go deeper, and a little personal, depending on the person and the situation. Based on the openers you used, you can build a chain of topics or questions that will help you know your conversation partner more, and build rapport.

For instance, if your opener topic talks about the event or the place, you can use the following questions as a guide:

This place is _____. I have been to _____ with a _____ similar to this. Where did you come from/Where do you live anyway?

8. Oh, that's too _____ from here. I'm from _____. That's where my parents live. But I stay at _____ here in the

city/State. Where do you stay?

9. You have a family there?

10. Did you go to (hometown) _____'s college/university?

11. What course did you take?

12. Where do you work now?

13. What kind of work do you do/What's your job position in that company?

Do you know the host/event organizer?

14. Oh, you do? How did you meet?

15. Oh, you don't. Well, I know him/her. He/She is _____. We _____. I think if you need a good host/organizer, you can put him/her on your list. Do you know anyone from here who's as good as him/her?

16. Do you think that events business is booming nowadays? I always see posts and

photos on Facebook/Instagram/Pinterest and I think they're gorgeous.

17. Do you know anyone who's into the same business?

18. Who would you recommend? Do you have their site or page/portfolio?

19. There's this _____ thing I heard/saw/experienced with an event's organizer. It was about _____. So _____ happened, and _____. Have you had the same experience? What happened?

This event is so _____. Have you ever been to a similar event before?

20. What was the most unforgettable moment you had in that event?

21. Well, you know, this kind of event is _____. I heard that _____. Can you believe that? What can you say about it?

22. Do you like/dislike how this event is progressing?

23. If there's one thing you would like to change in this event, what would it be? Why?

24. So, I've been in this event before, and this happened. You won't believe it. _____. Well, what do you think of that?

What brings you to this event by the way?

25. Do you know a lot of people here?

26. Well, I know the _____ of this event. He/She/They is/are my _____. Do you know him/her/them?

Well, the hor d'ouvres is _____! Did you like/hate it, too? What did you like/hate best/least?

27. I had this worst food experience. So, I was at _____ for the _____, then what

happened was _____.
How about you? What's your most unforgettable food experience?

28. All I can say is I'm an avid Food Guy/Girl. I waste my TV time watching these food videos on Channel _____. Do you watch them, too?

    <**Additional:** I kind of hate Gordon Ramsay's guts but you gotta give it to the man. He knows what he's doing. What about you? What can you say about him?>

29. I like to travel and try out different cuisines. I have been to _____ and the food was great. Have you been there before? Have you tried the _____? How do you feel about it?

    <**Additional:** Do you travel, too? What places have you visited before? What happened while you were there? Did you enjoy the food/tourist spots? I'm planning to visit _____, too soon. What place do

you recommend? Where's the best place to stay/visit?>

30. I just thought the weirdest thing. You see when I visited this joint/restaurant/diner in _____, they served _____. I know right? It's kind of weird. What's the weirdest food you ate?

What do you do/What's your job?

31. Oh, really? That sounds tough/interesting. So, what do you usually do as a/an _____ in your company?

32. What's your company? What does it mainly do?

33. Well, I'm a/an at my company. Basically, my company is _____ and my job there is to _____. Does your company have the same function/job designation? Do you have partners in the same line of business?

34. How long have you been working in _____? What made you stay there?

Where were you before? What made you quit?

35. In my case, I have been working in ____ for _____. I used to work in _____ as _____, but I decided to quit because_____. I quite like the _____ in my current work. How about you? What do you think is the main reason why employees stay loyal in one company?

36. If you're going to choose between pay and culture, what would it be? Why?

37. Well, you have a point there. I've just been reminded of one colleague who _____. He/She _____, then _____. How do you feel about that?

38. What's your most unforgettable work story?

As you can see, there are various interesting directions where your conversation can go, even if they begin from one starter topic. The secret is to be sincerely interested and enthused in knowing more about your conversation partner/s. That's why all follow-up questions should be directed towards your partner, even if they begin with telling something about yourself. The recommended pattern is: **I am/have _____. What about you/What do you think about it?**

Placing the ball in your conversation partner's court guarantees a longer, deeper and more meaningful response, instead of just getting a cutting Yes or No. This setup keeps the conversation flowing.

Ender/Exit

The ender is the second most difficult part of a conversation. When the discussion is so interesting and your group is having fun, you can't just cut it, or else you'll compromise your already established "likable impression." Whatever happens, you should have that graceful exit. How do you do that?

The secret is proper timing. If you need to be somewhere at a specific time, be sure that you are aware of the clock, and somehow have a plan on how to gracefully exit. It should be your turn in speaking before you end it, so you can say your goodbye politely.

You can nonchalantly look at your watch immediately after saying your piece, and say something like, *"Oh, look at how time flies! I was really having fun I didn't notice it. I need to go to _____ for _____."*

Always say thank you to your conversation partner for the enjoyable talk, and express your sincere hope of meeting them again in the future. In case that you want to get in touch with them soon for professional purposes such as business, leave a business card.

Art of Small Talk

As previously mentioned, small talk creates the groundwork for conversation build-up. It is an opportunity to establish good impressions and smooth flow of discussion. The art of small talk requires confidence and focus. With small talk, even the most mundane topics must become interesting, so the fate of the conversation lies heavily on the skills of the speaker. Any wrong move can result in awkwardness and possibly a disastrous aftermath.

Beginners can flex their conversation skills by going straight to small talk. It is actually the best arena for developing conversation skills, where you make errors, and find out your strengths and weaknesses. The following are examples of topics for small talk, which you can use to anyone, anytime, anywhere:

39. Weather

Yes, yes. Weather is a cliché topic for small talk. Its commonness is actually its charm, and the reason why it's universally expected to be the first in the list of small talk starters. It works almost all the time, so why not use it? Whether it's sunny, windy, or wintry, it's weather, and you can easily think of a dozen topics about it.

- Well I say, this constant rain of cats and dogs has been getting worse every day. I'm having problems getting my clothes dry, I don't know if I have a pair of pants to wear tomorrow. Do you think we might be seeing some ray of sunshine next week?

- Gosh, this snow is crazy! How's your car/pathway/roof? I thought I was getting out of an igloo when I walk out of my house this morning. I had to shovel ice from my pathway and car. Had any problem getting out today?

40. People

There is no limit to the number of topics you can come up for small talk when you look around. Case in point: People. There are billions of people in the world today, each with a different personality, different focus or subject of attention. So, when you see a person you want to strike a conversation with, take a look around and see what the other people are doing. Remember though: **Be Nice.**

- Would you look at that, how many dads today have much time to play with their daughters? You got kids? How many?

- See that guy over there? That's Mr. _____, an old baker across the street where I live. He makes these flaky croissants with cream fillings every single morning and sells them with free brewed coffee. It's fantastic. Have you tried them out before? Where do you buy your bread around here? Do you live near?

41. Sceneries

Similar to a variety of topics you can get by using people as subjects, your surroundings provide as many possible topics for small talks. You just have to be creative in picking one and focusing on it to come up with good follow-up topics/questions and keep the conversation smooth and flowing.

- This park is nice, right? Fresh air, lots of trees. You should see it during the fall. The leaves of those big trees near the lake turn red and burgundy in color. Are you from around here, by the way? Oh, where do you stay?/Oh, where are you from?

- See those birds over there? I heard that those migrate as far as _____ before the winter season. You know what they are called? Are you from around here?

- Brings back a lot of childhood memories?

Which one do you like most, the swings or the slide? You used to have one near your home when you're a kid? Got kids of your own?

42. Events/Seasons

Anything special about the season or an event such as a holiday, New Year's, etc. is an easy topic to start a small talk with anyone.

- It's that time of the year again, I guess. First time to spend Christmas here?

- Not much to do during Thanksgiving in this part of the city. How's Thanksgiving going on with the family?

43. Personal Experiences/Details

This one is rather tricky, and has the risk of sounding invasive of someone's privacy, especially if you're talking to a stranger. If you're adept in finding out a person's character by just a glimpse and short observation, then you can easily decide if you'll go straight to personal questions or not.

- You seem to be carrying the world in your shoulders, lad. Care to share what's bothering you?

- You look like a very interesting guy/girl. Care to tell me something about yourself?

44. Common Ground

It's quite easy to strike a conversation with a stranger when you have something common at that exact moment, say, attending the same event, being introduced by a common friend or drinking at the same bar. Aside from the ease and comfort felt by both parties, the topics to choose from are various and diverse.

- Hi, are you enjoying the conference? What engineering club are you in?

- How did you know Bob? He's been my friend for 10 years, and it's my first time meeting you.

45. Current Events

Current events such as what's happening in the news lately is an easy pick for small talk starters. Try to mellow down on the opinions, however, and again, practice empathy and patience.

- All these fuel hikes, you'd believe it's better to just get back to bikes and carriages. What do you think? How's it affecting you?

- Can't believe what's happening to Indonesia right now. Earthquakes like that are sure scary. Have you seen the news? Ever experienced a scare like that?

46. Work

Talks about work is a safe enough ground where both parties can be neutral and the flow of conversation leans more on descriptive rather than opinionated. Typical follow-up questions are queries about the company, including its type of business and culture (refer to items 31 – 38).

47. Sports/Games

Imagine that you're sitting in a bar, watching a football game while drinking a beer just like anyone else. Expectedly, the place will be energized and have a fun atmosphere, so it's quite easy to make some small talks with everyone. Watching a game in a stadium might be too noisy to create long discussions with peer spectators, but small talks are easy to make. The latest NBA playoff game with your favorite team playing, or the Olympics that has just started are good samples of small talk starters when your prospect conversation partner is a stranger, and you decided to get a conversation going in a "non-sport" place.

- Timberwolves won the last game. Yay! You into basketball? What's your team? Why do you like that team? Who's your favorite player?

48. Music

Music is a universal like, of all ages, every generation, every nation. It's quite difficult to encounter a person who hates music in general, so it's a safe enough topic for general conversation. Still, you'd need to look for things around that will fit into the music context. You can't just blurt out talks about music unless something at the moment can be linked to it. For instance, if you're in a coffee shop that plays an interesting bossa nova playlist, you can use that as a starter for music-oriented small talk.

- (Music playing in the background): This is a good song. Do you know its title? How about the artist? You don't seem/seem to be interested in this kind of genre, what genre are you into? Why do you like that? Do you have a music influence or something?

49. Hobbies and Crafts

Topics about arts, hobbies, and crafts are usually comfortable to use for small talks if you happen to be in an event or a place where similar hobbyists or artists are attending. It's a good opportunity to get interested in new things, probably try them out or learn about them while having fulfilling conversations with perfect strangers. It's also easy to endear yourself to other people and possibly gain friends or professional partners because you honestly act enthused as you try to learn more about other people's interests.

- I've always wanted to try beekeeping! I'm a sucker for pure, raw honey, but it's very difficult for me to do that. I live in the city, at a 10-storey building. How do you do it? Do you think it's possible to try that out in my place? How?

50. World Issues

World issues can be very sensitive topics. They require tact, courtesy, and empathy when being discussed with other people, especially strangers. Opinionated topics are good sources of long, fulfilling and smart conversations, but they can be tricky if (1) you're not familiar with the topic; (2) there is social diversity (ethnicity/race, religion, political leaning, etc.) involved; and (3) you have experiential lack/disadvantage. In such cases, the best way is to act as an empty vessel and a conduit, aside from the expected practice of tact and consideration, at all times.

By being in the middle ground, you're able to see

different sides of the story, multiple facets of an idea, and opposite perspectives of people. Not only do you gain knowledge about the topic, but friends as well. Furthermore, if unsure, always ask questions. It's better to admit ignorance but with a willingness to learn, rather than pretend that you know things.

51. Anything Under the Sun

Everything around us has its own different stories. Stories are always exciting treasures to discover, new places to explore, new experiments to tinker with. The quiet man you always pass by when you go to your favorite bakery, the little dog that barks at you at the park, the ancient tree standing at your neighbor's front yard – these are stories that are already made, yet you can make them or alter them or create something more out of them. The choice, the ways – they're endless.

Chapter Four: Flex Your Conversation Muscles

As cliché as it sounds, practice do make perfect, and conversation skills direly need a regular muscle-flexing to grow and develop. In the previous chapters, you have been taught about fear, including how to assess yours and bring it to manageable levels. You also have tips on how to start with small talks and progress in conversations, from starter to ender, right under your sleeve. Now it's time to apply what you've learned to the real world.

Breathe deeply. Relax. Begin the Introductions. Now here are some of the additional tips to remember while you're having conversations:

First-Name Basis

Saying the other person's name, or in case of

conversing with a group, the other people's names, puts them at ease and endears you to them. It shows that you make time to remember their names and are sincere in really knowing them.

Just Yes or No is a No-no

A single "yes" or "no" for an answer is a roadblock both parties will have trouble in overcoming. It's awkward, especially if no follow-up question arises. Be creative in the next questions you will ask. Make them talk longer. When they ask you a question, end your answer with a question, too.

Be Natural

Humans are naturally smart in getting the subtexts, reading non-verbal cues, and finding out more thru instincts. Be honest and sincere from the very beginning, and you can easily break someone's wall.

Conclusion: Going Beyond with the Power of Conversation

Assertiveness is one of the major pillars of communication. As mentioned, it is putting across, in a nice and proper way, your needs and desires in the conversation. It's your way of not being left out in the conversation. Hence, in a way, you should exert control and dominance on the conversation, and where it goes. This is called influence, which is driven by the following factors: emotion, expertise, positional power, and control over the interaction *(Source: Nick Morgan, Conversation and Extend Your Influence,*

https://www.forbes.com/sites/nickmorgan/2013/04/25/how-you-can-dominate-the-conversation-and-extend-your-influence/#264bf36b7ba0).

Emotion

Nick Morgan emphasizes the use of passion to influence the flow of conversation. In fact, passion can sway people, as we are emotional beings. Despite power and position, there is a heart that works there somewhere, that responds to emotions and listens to empathetic pleas. Passion with patience, in particular choosing the right moment to speak and when to leave a lasting impression, is a powerful tool.

Expertise

Passion is more powerful if you put expertise on the mix. Expertise strengthens confidence, and confidence gives a person more voice – the power to be heard. However, confidence can be dangerously used to cover up ignorance, and expertise without confidence pushes you to the back door.

Positional Power

Positional power gives a person an edge, the expected right to speak and dominate a conversation. People knows and respects authority, and that automatically offers the floor for leading a conversation.

Interaction

Even if it's the subtlest aspect of influence, it is the most difficult to master, and perhaps the strongest of the four. In fact, this aspect can be easily used to manipulate, not only the conversation but also the people involved, their responses and reactions. This aspect doesn't just make use the power of words, but the ability to read non-verbal cues, especially body languages. The secret of this aspect is the understanding of people in general – what makes them tick, what makes them disagreeable – and using this to create a conversation that is harmonious, fulfilling, and interesting, yet still largely under your control.

James W. Williams

Thank you!

Before you go, I just wanted to say thank you for purchasing my book.

You could have picked from dozens of other books on the same topic but you took a chance and chose this one.

So, a HUGE thanks to you for getting this book and for reading all the way to the end.

Now I wanted to ask you for a small favor. **Could you please consider posting a review on the platform? Reviews are one of the easiest ways to support the work of independent authors.**

This feedback will help me continue to write the type of books that will help you get the results you want. So if you enjoyed it, please let me know! (-:

Go to this link to leave a review!

https://www.amazon.com/review/create-review/

Lastly, don't forget to grab a copy of your Free Bonus book *"Bulletproof Confidence Checklist"*. If you want to learn how to overcome shyness and social anxiety and become more confident then this book is for you.

Just go to:

https://theartofmastery.com/confidence/

www.ingramcontent.com/pod-product-compliance
Lightning Source LLC
Chambersburg PA
CBHW052105110526
44591CB00013B/2355